NEW POEMS ON
THE UNDERGROUND
2006

also published by Cassell

POEMS ON THE UNDERGROUND

10TH EDITION

NEW
POEMS ON THE
UNDERGROUND
2006

EDITED BY

Gerard Benson · Judith Chernaik · Cicely Herbert

CASSELL

Cassell

The Orion Publishing Group Ltd
Orion House
5 Upper Saint Martin's Lane, London WC2H 9EA

This edition first published 2006

1 3 5 7 9 10 8 6 4 2

British Library Cataloguing-in-Publication Data
A catalogue record for this book is available from the British Library

ISBN-13: 978-0-30436-814-3
ISBN-10: 0-304-36814-8

Designed by Gwyn Lewis

Printed and bound in Italy

www.orionbooks.co.uk

The Orion Publishing Group policy is to use papers that are natural,
renewable and recyclable products and made from wood grown in
sustainable forests. The logging and manufacturing processes are expected
to conform to the environmental regulations of the country of origin.

CONTENTS

INTRODUCTION

Just over twenty years ago we wrote to London Underground proposing that empty advertising spaces in Tube carriages be filled with poems. The response was cautious but positive, and Poems on the Underground was born.

London Underground, which has supported us ever since, has a long history of design excellence, going back to Henry Beck's Tube map and the distinctive Johnston typeface. In the early days of the Underground, stations were enlivened by posters advertising the countryside and the West End, which had become easily accessible by cheap transport. Posters often included a few lines of poetry Keats or Shelley for the countryside, Wordsworth, less obviously, for Oxford Street ("Getting and spending, we lay waste our powers").

Last year's terrorist attacks on London's transport system have affected the city and the Underground in ways we can hardly bear to think about. But we hope that the Tube poems can continue to be a source of diversion, even consolation, for travellers. For poetry retains its power in difficult times. Indeed, it could be argued that people turn to poetry even more when their usual assumptions about life are overturned; if "poetry makes nothing happen," as Auden wrote, it often offers ways of understanding the troubled present and its relation to an equally troubled past.

The poets represented in this volume, from Chaucer and Shakespeare to Blake and Yeats, lived in times as violent as our own; many of the twentieth-century European and Commonwealth poets included here actively participated in the upheavals afflicting their countries. All these poets lament the carnage of war and tyranny, and celebrate the enduring human values – "the miraculous continuity of little motions" (Yannis Ritsos), the "Eternal spirit of the chainless mind" (Byron).

New Poems 2006, celebrating our twentieth anniversary year, brings our entire collection up to date, adding twenty-six poems to

New Poems 2004. The tenth edition of our earlier collection, *Poems on the Underground* (2001), includes more than 300 poems. The additional 'New Poems' include a special display of four Chinese poems, drawn from two thousand continuous years of Chinese poetry, part of an exchange of poems with Shanghai Metro. We also include two sets of poems by 'Young Poets', winners of the Poetry Society's competitions for young people.

In all other respects we have gone on pretty much as we began, selecting short poems (occasionally extracts) from the earliest times to the present, in the hope that a captive audience of millions will take pleasure in poems placed in no particular order in random Tube carriages. Our general policy remains the same; we include at least two living poets in each display, and try to reach a balance between the familiar and the relatively unknown, trawling happily through poems of all times and places.

Translations have a special place in our collection, reflecting the interest English poets have always had in other languages and cultures, from Chaucer's translation of the French 'Romance of the Rose' and Shakespeare's free use of Plutarch to Coleridge 'plagiarising' Schiller. In turn, Shakespeare's words, translated into every world language, have inspired Italian opera, Russian ballet and Japanese film; while the passionate defence of liberty by Milton, Blake and Shelley has been echoed by people across Europe and beyond.

London remains our centre, and as one might expect, the city itself is a chief character in several poems – 'The London Eye', 'Homage to the British Museum', and (flatteringly) 'Poem on the Underground'. London has always been the home of poets, many of whom pay tribute to the city in their works. Marlowe, Donne, Keats and Isaac Rosenberg all experienced the best and worst of London life in their time. London's open-air folk poetry was featured in our commission for the City of London Festival: Evelyn Ficarra's 'London Cries', which sets taped sounds of London street markets alongside Elizabethan market cries immortalised by Orlando Gibbons. Another special commission, new poems by poets featured on the Tube for *Carnival of the Animals,* has just been published by Walker Books, with illustrations by Satoshi Kitamura and a CD of Saint-Saëns' music, performed by the Apollo Chamber Players. And to mark our twentieth anniversary, Cassell has just released a CD of readings from *Poems on the Underground* by eleven poets whose poems appear in our collection.

During the past five years, we've given poetry readings, usually connected to our choice of poems, at Conway Hall, the Italian Cultural Institute, Keats House, the British Library, and St Michael's Church Highgate, where Coleridge is buried (a reading of *The Ancient Mariner*, with piano accompaniment adapted from Wagner's *Flying Dutchman*). In the British Museum Reading Room, that superb domed metaphor for the human brain, we performed Blake's *Songs of Innocence and of Experience*, with slides of Blake's original hand-coloured images and music by Vaughan Williams – a true celebration of the sister arts of music, painting and poetry.

Similar programmes of 'public' poetry continue to spring up across the world, most recently in Shanghai. Porto and Helsinki have displayed bilingual and even trilingual poems on their public transport systems, including some of our selections. And programmes begun in response to ours in Dublin, Stuttgart, Paris, New York, Stockholm, Prague, Vienna, Athens, and many other cities continue to thrive. It may be wishful thinking, but we hope this reflects a hunger for poetry on the part of people everywhere.

Since the inception of Poems on the Underground we have been London based, though posters of the poems reach schools and libraries across Britain and abroad. Our choice of poems is always made with the London traveller in mind, especially the traveller on the Underground. We try to keep a sense of perspective, recognising that posters, even of great poetry, are ephemeral, and public art a modest element in the urban scene. Still, every now and then a poem seems particularly appropriate, especially as our selection reappears in book form. Some years ago we displayed a poem by the great Polish poet Czeslaw Milosz, 'And Yet the Books', which we displayed again, more recently, to mark Poland's entry into the European Union. Now as when it was

written, more than twenty years ago, it beautifully defines the function
of literature in uncertain times:

And yet the books will be there on the shelves, separate beings,
That appeared once, still wet
As shining chestnuts, under a tree in autumn,
And, touched, coddled, began to live
In spite of fires on the horizon, castles blown up,
Tribes on the march, planets in motion.
"We are," they said, even as their pages
Were being torn out, or a buzzing flame
Licked away their letters. So much more durable
Than we are, whose frail warmth
Cools down with memory, disperses, perishes.
I imagine the earth when I am no more:
Nothing happens, no loss, it's still a strange pageant,
Women's dresses, dewy lilacs, a song in the valley.
Yet the books will be there on the shelves, well born,
Derived from people, but also from radiance, heights.

CZESLAW MILOSZ (1911–2004)
translated by CZESLAW MILOSZ *and* ROBERT HASS

Gerard Benson, Judith Chernaik, Cicely Herbert
LONDON 2006

THE POEMS

Song

Whenas the rye reach to the chin,
And chopcherry, chopcherry ripe within,
Strawberries swimming in the cream,
And schoolboys playing in the stream:
Then O, then O, then O, my true love said,
Till that time come again,
She could not live a maid.

from THE OLD WIVES' TALE

GEORGE PEELE (1556–96)

from The Rime of the Ancient Mariner

Beyond the shadow of the ship,
I watched the water-snakes:
They moved in tracks of shining white,
And when they reared, the elfish light
Fell off in hoary flakes.

Within the shadow of the ship
I watched their rich attire:
Blue, glossy green, and velvet black,
They coiled and swam; and every track
Was a flash of golden fire.

O happy living things! no tongue
Their beauty might declare:
A spring of love gushed from my heart,
And I blessed them unaware:
Sure my kind saint took pity on me,
And I blessed them unaware.

The self-same moment I could pray;
And from my neck so free
The Albatross fell off, and sank
Like lead into the sea.

PART 4, LINES 272–291

SAMUEL TAYLOR COLERIDGE (1772–1834)

The Rime of the Ancient Mariner 'Beyond the shadow of the ship, I watched the water-snakes', an illustration by Gustave Doré from his 1876 edition of Samuel Taylor Coleridge's epic tale. Doré's signature is opposite that of his engraver, Jonnard, at the foot.

They Are Not Long

*Vitae summa brevis spem nos vetat incohare longam**

They are not long, the weeping and the laughter,
    Love and desire and hate:
I think they have no portion in us after
    We pass the gate.

They are not long, the days of wine and roses:
    Out of a misty dream
Our path emerges for a while, then closes
    Within a dream.

ERNEST DOWSON (1867–1900)

*Life's short span prevents us from entertaining far-off hopes (Horace)

Should You Die First

Let me at least collect your smells
as specimens: your armpits, woollen sweater,
fingers yellow from smoke. I'd need
to take an imprint of your foot
and make recordings of your laugh.

These archives I shall carry into exile;
my body a St Helena where ships no longer dock,
a rock in the ocean, an outpost where the wind howls
and polar bears beat down the door.

ANNABELLE DESPARD (b. 1943)

New Gravity

Treading through the half-light of ivy
and headstone, I see you in the distance
as I'm telling our daughter
about this place, this whole business:
a sister about to be born,
how a life's new gravity suspends in water.
Under the oak, the fallen leaves
are pieces of the tree's jigsaw;
by your father's grave you are pressing acorns
into the shadows to seed.

ROBIN ROBERTSON (b. 1955)

giovanni caboto/john cabot

fourteen hundred and ninety seven
giovanni sailed from the coast of devon

   52 days   discovered cape breton n.s.
   caught some cod   went home
   with 10 bear hides
   (none prime)

   told henry 7
   his majesty now owned
   cipango   land of jewels
   abounding moreover in silks
   & brasilwode
   also the spice islands of asia
   & the country of the grand khan

   henry gave giovanni 30 quid
   to go back to nova scotia

who was kidding who?

          EARLE BIRNEY (1904–95)

Greek Antiquities: First Floor

Little sculptured animals, young deer
still stiffly running, still with bright
and frightened eyes, my fingers touch
the tiny perforations that mark
the spots upon your coats of clay
and find them rough and hard. Will any
dream of mine so run, wakeful
through more than twenty centuries?

LAURIS EDMOND (1924–2000)

Ibadan

Ibadan,
       running splash of rust
and gold – flung and scattered
among seven hills like broken
china in the sun.

J.P. CLARK-BEKEDEREMO (b. 1935)

Architecture

The architecture of an aunt
Made the child dream of cupolas,
Domes, other smoothly rondured shapes.
Geometries troubled his sleep.

The architecture of young women
Mildly obsessed the young man:
Its globosity, firmness, texture,
Lace cobwebs for adornment and support.

Miles from his aunt, the old child
Watched domes and cupolas defaced
In a hundred countries, as time passed.

A thousand kilometres of lace defiled,
And much gleaming and perfect architecture
Flaming in the fields with no visible support.

DOM MORAES (1938–2004)

The Palm Trees at Chigawe

You stood like women in green
Proud travellers in panama hats and java print
Your fruit-milk caused monkeys and shepherds to scramble
Your dry leaves were banners for night fishermen
But now stunted trees stand still beheaded –
A curious sight for the tourists

JACK MAPANJE (b. 1944)

Viv

for cricketer, Vivian Richards

Like the sun rising and setting
Like the thunderous roar of a bull rhino
Like the sleek, quick grace of a gazelle,
The player springs into the eye
And lights the world with fires
Of a million dreams, a million aspirations.
The batsman-hero climbs the skies,
Strikes the earth-ball for six
And the landscape rolls with the ecstasy of the magic play.

Through the covers, the warrior thrusts a majestic cut
Lighting the day with runs
As bodies reel and tumble,
Hands clap, eyes water
And hearts move inside out.

The volcano erupts!
Blows the game apart.

FAUSTIN CHARLES (b. 1944)

Free

Born free
to be caught
and fashioned
and shaped
and freed to wander
within
a caged dream
of tears

MERLE COLLINS (b. 1950)

Indian Cooking

The bottom of the pan was a palette –
paprika, cayenne, dhania
haldi, heaped like powder-paints.

Melted ghee made lakes, golden rivers.
The keema frying, my mother waited
for the fat to bubble to the surface.

Friends brought silver-leaf.
I dropped it on khir –
special rice pudding for parties.

I tasted the landscape, customs
of my father's country –
its fever on biting a chilli.

MONIZA ALVI (b. 1954)

A Tune

A foolish rhythm turns in my idle head
As a wind-mill turns in the wind on an empty sky.
Why is it when love, which men call deathless, is dead,
That memory, men call fugitive, will not die?
Is love not dead? Yet I hear that tune if I lie
Dreaming awake in the night on my lonely bed,
And an old thought turns with the old tune in my head
As a wind-mill turns in the wind on an empty sky.

ARTHUR SYMONS (1865–1945)

Fine Knacks for Ladies Lines from John Dowland's *Second Booke of Songs or Ayres*, 1600. By permission of the British Library.

Fine Knacks for Ladies

Fine knacks for ladies, cheap, choice, brave and new;
  Good pennyworths but money cannot move.
I keep a fair but for the fair to view.
  A beggar may be liberal of love;
Though all my wares be trash, the heart is true.

Great gifts are guiles and look for gifts again;
  My trifles come as treasures from my mind.
It is a precious jewel to be plain.
  Sometimes in shell the orient'st pearls we find;
Of others take a sheaf, of me a grain.

Within this pack pins, points, laces and gloves,
  And divers toys fitting a country fair;
But in my heart, where duty serves and loves,
  Turtles and twins, court's brood, a heavenly pair.
Happy the heart that thinks of no removes!

ANON. (before 1600)

Sonnet on Chillon

Eternal spirit of the chainless mind!
  Brightest in dungeons, Liberty! thou art,
  For there thy habitation is the heart –
The heart which love of thee alone can bind;
And when thy sons to fetters are consigned,
  To fetters, – and the damp vault's dayless gloom,
  Their country conquers with their martyrdom,
And Freedom's fame finds wings on every wind.
Chillon! thy prison is a holy place,
  And thy sad floor an altar – for 'twas trod
Until his very steps have left a trace
  Worn, as if thy cold pavement were a sod,
By Bonnivard! – may none those marks efface!
  For they appeal from tyranny to God.

GEORGE GORDON, LORD BYRON (1788–1824)

Sonnet on Chillon Byron's manuscript, by
permission of the John Murray Archive.

Sonnet on Chillon

Eternal Spirit of the chainless Mind!
　Brightest in dungeons — Liberty! thou art,
For there thy habitation is the heart
The heart which Love of thee alone can bind,
And when thy sons to fetters are consigned,
　To fetters — and the damp vaults' dayless gloom,
Their Country conquers with their Martyrdom,
And Freedom's fame finds wings on every Wind. —
Chillon! thy prison is a holy place,
　And thy sad floor an Altar — for 'twas trod
Until his very steps have left a trace
　Worn, as if thy cold pavement were a Sod,
By Bonnivard! — may none those marks efface!
For they appeal from Tyranny to God. —

Accordionist

for André Kertész

The accordionist is a blind intellectual
carrying an enormous typewriter whose keys
grow wings as the instrument expands into a tall
horizontal hat that collapses with a tubercular wheeze.

My century is a sad one of collapses.
The concertina of the chest; the tubular bells
of the high houses; the flattened ellipses
of our skulls that open like petals.

We are the poppies sprinkled along the field.
We are simple crosses dotted with blood.
Beware the sentiments concealed
in this short rhyme. Be wise. Be good.

GEORGE SZIRTES (b. 1948)

Notes from a Tunisian Journal

This nutmeg stick of a boy in loose trousers!
Little coffee pots in the coals, a mint on the tongue.

The camels stand in all their vague beauty –
at night they fold up like pale accordions.

All the hedges are singing with yellow birds!
A boy runs by with lemons in his hands.

Food's perfume, breath is nourishment.
The stars crumble, salt above eucalyptus fields.

RITA DOVE (b. 1952)

I am thinking of a Jewish play
with Judas Macabeas for hero.
I can put a lot in I've learnt
out here   I hope I get the
chance to go on with it.   I've
~~just~~ written this thing — red from the
anvil
                Aug 1914.
What in our lives is burnt
In the fire of this?
The heart's dear granary?
The much we shall miss?
Three lives hath one life —
Iron, honey, gold.
The gold, the honey gone —
Left is the hard & cold.
Iron are our lives
Molten right through our youth.
A burnt space through ripe fields,
A fair month's broken tooth.
I have a good one in the anvil now, but
it wants knocking into shape.
Thanks very much for the paper.
            Yours sincerely Isaac Rosenberg

August 1914

What in our lives is burnt
In the fire of this?
The heart's dear granary?
The much we shall miss?

Three lives hath one life –
Iron, honey, gold.
The gold, the honey gone –
Left is the hard and cold.

Iron are our lives
Molten right through our youth.
A burnt space through ripe fields,
A fair mouth's broken tooth.

ISAAC ROSENBERG (1890–1918)

August 1914 An extract from the poet's letter to Mrs Herbert Cohen, in which he includes 'red from the anvil' the text of his new poem. By permission of the Imperial War Museum, IR/I/236, and the Literary Executors of Mrs A. Wynick.

Under the Stairs

She has a small shop under the stairs
where I buy black beads and velvet cloth
and the little pleasures of a shiny green apple sticker.

But I am older now and I act as if I don't
remember what it was like to pretend
because she is my sister and I am alone.

The blue airplane has no wheels.
The bucket filled with yellow stars
has no handle. The pinwheel does not turn.

I like those best because they are like me.

CAITLIN McLEOD

Dockside

Sat by the water for hours. Watched nothing but water,
how it was spelt out by light;

its mass like silk blown in slow-moving wind,

      or the glitter of fisted diamonds that flickered and
                        kicked
      as the waves caught the light
      from the bounce of the sun and I squinted my eyes
                      and saw every one

      of those diamonds that tickled and swam,

      or how the light lay like a curve
      in a ripple of time, on that wet pool
      and I thought of a painter
      jig-sawing brushstrokes of yellow
      over the salty-sea blue.

AMNA AHMED

The End of Every Field

She calls me a wild horse.
Either that or I'm a kite breaking from its string.
This is when she is angry and sees me
Galloping to the end of
Every field before levitating into
The sky and herself
With a stunned empty
Rope in her hand
Like the one they scissored
When my breakable child bones
Came pushing from her years ago.

QIAN XI TENG

from **Inferno**

In the middle of the journey of our life
  I found myself astray in a dark wood
  where the right road had been lost sight of.
How hard it is to say what it was like
  in the thick of thickets, in a wood so dense and gnarled
  the very thought of it renews my panic.
It is bitter almost as death itself is bitter.
  But to rehearse the good it also brought me
  I will speak about the other things I saw there.

    Nel mezzo del cammin di nostra vita
      mi ritrovai per una selva oscura,
      ché la diritta via era smarrita.
    Ah quanto a dir qual era è cosa dura
      esta selva selvaggia e aspra e forte
      che nel pensier rinnova la paura!
    Tant'è amara che poco è più morte;
      ma per trattar del ben ch'io vi trovai,
      dirò de l'altre cose ch'io v'ho scorte.

CANTO I, 1-9

DANTE ALIGHIERI (1265–1321)
translated by SEAMUS HEANEY

'The waves, blue walls'

The waves, blue walls
of Africa, go and come back.

When they go. . .
Ah, to go with them!

Ah, to come back with them!
When they come back . . .

'Murallas azules, olas'

Murallas azules, olas,
del Africa, van y vienen.

Cuando van . . .
¡Ay, quién con ellas se fuera!

¡Ay, quién con ellas volviera!
Cuando vuelven. . .

from MARINERO EN TIERRA

RAFAEL ALBERTI (1902–99)
translated by MARK STRAND

From **Marinero en Tierra** Woodcut by Rafael Alberti, one
of many illustrations from his book of poems *Marinero en
Tierra* (1924). By permission of El Alba del Alhelí, S. L.

Miracle

A man, before going to bed, put his watch under his pillow.
Then he went to sleep. Outside the wind was blowing. You
 who know
the miraculous continuity of little motions, understand.
A man, his watch, the wind. Nothing else.

Θαύμα

Ενας άνθρωπος, προτού πλαγιάσει, έβαλε το
 ρολόι του κάτω απ' το προσκέφαλό του.
Υστερα κοιμήθηκε. Κ' έξω φυσούσε. Εσύ που ξέρεις
τη θαυμαστή συνέχεια των μικρών κινήσεων,
 καταλαβαινεις.
Ενας άνθρωπος, το ρολόι του, ο άνεμος. Τίποτ' άλλο.

YANNIS RITSOS (1909–90)
translated by RAE DALVEN

In the Poem

To bring the picture the wall the wind
The flower the glass the shine on wood
And the cold chaste clearness of water
To the clean severe world of the poem

To save from death decay and ruin
The actual moment of vision and surprise
And keep in the real world
The real gesture of a hand touching the table.

No Poema

Transferir o quadro o muro a brisa
A flor o copo o brilho da madeira
E a fria e virgem limpidez da água
Para o mundo do poema limpo e rigoroso

Preservar de decadência morte e ruína
O instante real de aparição e de surpresa
Guardar num mundo claro
O gesto claro da mão tocando a mesa.

SOPHIA DE MELLO BREYNER (b. 1919)
translated by RUTH FAINLIGHT

'Let a place be made'

Let a place be made for the one who draws near,
The one who is cold, deprived of any home,

Tempted by the sound of a lamp, by the lit
Threshold of a solitary house.

And if he is still exhausted, full of anguish,
Say again for him those words that heal.

What does this heart which once was silence need
If not those words which are both sign and prayer,

Like a fire caught sight of in the sudden night,
Like the table glimpsed in a poor house?

'Qu'une place soit faite'

Qu'une place soit faite à celui qui approche,
Personnage ayant froid et privé de maison.

Personnage tenté par le bruit d'une lampe,
Par le seuil éclairé d'une seule maison.

Et s'il reste recru d'angoisse et de fatigue,
Qu'on redise pour lui les mots de guérison.

Que faut-il à ce cœur qui n'était que silence,
Sinon des mots qui soient le signe et l'oraison,

Et comme un peu de feu soudain la nuit,
Et la table entrevue d'une pauvre maison?

YVES BONNEFOY (b. 1923)
translated by ANTHONY RUDOLF

The Aegean

This music has lasted since the world began.
A rock was born among the waters
while tiny waves chatted in a soft universal tongue.
The shell of a sea-turtle
would not have foretold the guitar.
Your music has always risen to the sky,
green taproot, Mother Sea,
first of all firsts. You enfold us,
nurturing us with music – threat,
fable, hypnosis, lullaby, roar,
omen, myth,
                little agonies
of grit, of wreckages, of joys –

Egeo

Dal principio del mondo dura questa musica.
Nacque fra acque un sasso,
chiacchieravano ondine in morbido esperanto.
Non avrebbe previsto la chitarra
un guscio di testuggine marina.
Da sempre sale al cielo la tua musica,
verde radice prima, mamma-mare,
prima di tutti i prima. Ci avviluppi
nutrendoci di musica – minaccia,
favola, ipnosi, ninnananna, rombo,
presagio, mito,
                piccole agonie
di graniglie, relitti, di allegrie –

MARIA LUISA SPAZIANI (b. 1924)
translated by BEVERLY ALLEN

Bonnard

Colour of rooms. Pastel shades. Crowds. Torsos at ease in
brilliant baths. And always, everywhere the light.

This is a way of creating the world again, of seeing
differences, of piling shadow on shadow, of showing up
distances, of bringing close, bringing close.

A way of furnishing too, of making yourself feel at home –
and others. Pink, flame, coral, yellow, magenta – extreme
colours for ordinary situations. This is a way to make a
new world.

Then watch it. Let the colours dry, let the carpets collect
a little dust. Let the walls peel gently, and people come,
innocent, nude, eager for bed or bath.

They look newmade too, these bodies, newborn and
innocent. Their flesh-tints fit the bright walls and floors
and they take a bath as if entering the first stream, the
first fountain.

ELIZABETH JENNINGS (1926–2001)

Almost without Noticing

Almost without noticing,
without thinking, it seems,
you've arrived where you see far.
Thirty years back, more, the path vanishes,
thirty years ahead, more, the path vanishes:
and you're forced to sit down in your own shadow
to think.
Memory,
mother of truth and myth,
tell how the terrain divided the stream.

Melkein huomaamatta

Niin kuin melkein huomaamatta, ajattelematta
olisi tullut paikkaan josta näkyy kauas.
Yli kolmekymmentä vuotta häipyy polkuna taakse
yli kolmekymmentä vuotta häipyy polkuna eteen
ja on pakko istahtaa itsensä varjoon
miettimään.
Kerro muisti,
toden ja tarun äiti
miten maasto jakoi virran.

EIRA STENBERG (b. 1943)
translated by HERBERT LOMAS

Optimistisches Liedchen

Hie und da kommt es vor,
daß einer um Hilfe schreit.
Schon springt ein andrer ins Wasser,
vollkommen kostenlos.

Mitten im dicksten Kapitalismus
kommt die schimmernde Feuerwehr
um die Ecke und löscht, oder im Hut
des Bettlers silbert es plötzlich.

Vormittags wimmelt es auf den Straßen
von Personen, die ohne gezücktes Messer
hin – und herlaufen, seelenruhig,
auf der Suche nach Milch und Radieschen.

Wie im tiefsten Frieden.

Ein herrlicher Anblick.

Optimistic Little Poem

Now and then it happens
that somebody shouts for help
and somebody else jumps in at once
and absolutely gratis.

Here in the thick of the grossest capitalism
round the corner comes the shining fire brigade
and extinguishes, or suddenly
there's silver in the beggar's hat.

Mornings the streets are full
of people hurrying here and there without
daggers in their hands, quite equably
after milk or radishes.

As though in a time of deepest peace.

A splendid sight.

HANS MAGNUS ENZENSBERGER (b. 1929)
translated by DAVID CONSTANTINE

from The Anniversary

All Kings, and all their favourites,
All glory of honours, beauties, wits,
The Sun itself, which makes times, as they pass,
Is elder by a year now than it was
When thou and I first one another saw:
All other things to their destruction draw,
  Only our love hath no decay;
This, no tomorrow hath, nor yesterday,
Running it never runs from us away,
But truly keeps his first, last, everlasting day.

JOHN DONNE (1572–1631)

The Negro Speaks of Rivers

I've known rivers:
I've known rivers ancient as the world and older than the
        flow of human blood in human veins.

My soul has grown deep like the rivers.

I bathed in the Euphrates when dawns were young.
I built my hut near the Congo and it lulled me to sleep.
I looked upon the Nile and raised the pyramids above it.
I heard the singing of the Mississippi when Abe Lincoln
        went down to New Orleans, and I've seen its
        muddy bosom turn all golden in the sunset.

I've known rivers:
Ancient, dusky rivers.

My soul has grown deep like the rivers.

LANGSTON HUGHES (1902–67)

Homage to the British Museum

There is a Supreme God in the ethnological section;
A hollow toad shape, faced with a blank shield.
He needs his belly to include the Pantheon,
Which is inserted through a hole behind.
At the navel, at the points formally stressed, at the organs
   of sense,
Lice glue themselves, dolls, local deities,
His smooth wood creeps with all the creeds of the world.

Attending there let us absorb the cultures of nations
And dissolve into our judgement all their codes.
Then, being clogged with a natural hesitation
(People are continually asking one the way out),
Let us stand here and admit that we have no road.
Being everything, let us admit that is to be something,
Or give ourselves the benefit of the doubt;
Let us offer our pinch of dust all to this God,
And grant his reign over the entire building.

WILLIAM EMPSON (1906–84)

The Polynesian god A'a The subject of William Empson's
poem, this wooden carving in the British Museum is illustrated
here in a drawing specially commissioned from the artist by
Poems on the Underground. © Laurie Lipton 2004.

Coda

Maybe we knew each other better
When the night was young and unrepeated
And the moon stood still over Jericho.

So much for the past; in the present
There are moments caught between heart-beats
When maybe we know each other better.

But what is that clinking in the darkness?
Maybe we shall know each other better
When the tunnels meet beneath the mountain.

LOUIS MacNEICE (1907–63)

Poetry

Who broke these mirrors
and tossed them
shard
by shard
among the branches?
And now . . .
shall we ask L'Akhdar to come and see?
Colours are all muddled up
and the image is entangled
with the thing
and the eyes burn.
L'Akhdar must gather these mirrors
on his palm
and match the pieces together
any way he likes
and preserve
the memory of the branch.

SAADI YOUSSEF (b. 1934)

translated from the Arabic by KHALED MATTAWA

The London Eye

Through my gold-tinted Gucci sunglasses,
the sightseers. Big Ben's quarter chime
strikes the convoy of number 12 buses
that bleeds into the city's monochrome.

Through somebody's zoom lens, me shouting
to you, 'Hello . . . on . . . bridge . . . 'minster!'
The aerial view postcard, the man writing
squat words like black cabs in rush hour.

The South Bank buzzes with a rising treble.
You kiss my cheek, formal as a blind date.
We enter Cupid's Capsule, a thought bubble
where I think, 'Space age!', you think, 'She was late.'

Big Ben strikes six, my SKIN.Beat blinks, replies
18.02. We're moving anti-clockwise.

PATIENCE AGBABI (b. 1965)

Sonnet 65

Since brass, nor stone, nor earth, nor boundless sea,
But sad mortality o'ersways their power,
How with this rage shall beauty hold a plea,
Whose action is no stronger than a flower?
O how shall summer's honey breath hold out
Against the wrackful siege of batt'ring days,
When rocks impregnable are not so stout,
Nor gates of steel so strong, but Time decays?
O fearful meditation! where, alack,
Shall Time's best jewel from Time's chest lie hid?
Or what strong hand can hold his swift foot back,
Or who his spoil of beauty can forbid?
   O none, unless this miracle have might,
   That in black ink my love may still shine bright.

WILLIAM SHAKESPEARE (1564–1616)

'I have a young sister' Fifteenth-century manuscript, the
earliest known record of this song. BL MS Sloane 2593,
ff.11,11v. By permission of the British Library.

'I have a young sister'

I have a young sister far beyond the sea
many be the druries that she sent me

she sent me the cherry without any stone
and so she did the dove without any bone

she sent me the briar without any rind
she bade me love my leman without longing

how should any cherry be without stone
and how should any dove be without bone

how should any briar be without rind
how should any love my leman without longing

when the cherry was a flower then had it no stone
when the dove was an egg then had it no bone

when the briar was unbred then had it no rind
when the maiden hath that she loveth she is without longing

ANON. (early 15th century)

druries: love-gifts   *leman:* sweetheart   *unbred:* unborn

Infant Joy

I have no name
I am but two days old.—
What shall I call thee?
I happy am
Joy is my name.—
Sweet joy befall thee!

Pretty joy!
Sweet joy but two days old.
Sweet joy I call thee;
Thou dost smile,
I sing the while—
Sweet joy befall thee!

WILLIAM BLAKE (1757–1827)

Dream

I am become a stranger to my dreams,
Their places unknown. A bridge there was
Over the lovely waters of the Tyne, my mother
Was with me, we were almost there,
It seemed, but in that almost opened up a valley
Extending and expanding, wind-sculptured sand;
Dry its paths, a beautiful waterless waste
Without one green leaf, sand-coloured behind closed eyes.
That film shifts, but the arid place remains
When day returns. Yet we were still going towards the Tyne,
That green river-side where childhood's flowers
Were growing still, my mother and I, she dead,
With me for ever in that dream.

KATHLEEN RAINE (1908–2003)

Exodus

For all mothers in anguish
Pushing out their babies
In a small basket

To let the river cradle them
And kind hands find
And nurture them

Providing safety
In a hostile world:
Our constant gratitude.

As in this last century
The crowded trains
Taking us away from home

Became our baby baskets
Rattling to foreign parts
Our exodus from death.

LOTTE KRAMER (b. 1923)

The bee dance

Let the grey dust thicken on the landings,
let the spiders tick in the wall,
let the locks rust and the keys be lost.

This is the yellow hive of my skull
where the bees dance on the honeycomb
their tales of direction and distance.

They tell how high the sun is, how far
to sweet marjoram, borage and thyme,
and the tall green masts of the sunflowers.

KEN SMITH (1938–2003)

Emmonsails Heath in winter

I love to see the old heaths withered brake
Mingle its crimpled leaves with furze & ling
While the old heron from the lonely lake
Starts slow & flaps his melancholly wing
& oddling crow in idle motions swing
On the half rotten ash trees topmost twig
Beside whose trunk the gipsey makes his bed
Up flies the bouncing woodcock from the brig
Where a black quagmire quakes beneath the tread
The fieldfare chatters in the whistling thorn
& for the awe round fields & closen rove
& coy bumbarrels twenty in a drove
Flit down the hedgerows in the frozen plain
& hang on little twigs & start again

Emmonsails Heath in Winter John Clare's original manuscript.
By permission of Peterborough Museum and Art Gallery.

Emmonsails Heath in Winter

I love to see the old heaths withered brake
Mingle its crimpled leaves with furze and ling
While the old heron from the lonely lake
Starts slow and flaps his melancholly wing
And oddling crow in idle motions swing
On the half rotten ash trees topmost twig
Beside whose trunk the gipsey makes his bed
Up flies the bouncing woodcock from the brig
Where a black quagmire quakes beneath the tread
The fieldfare chatters in the whistling thorn
And for the awe round fields and closen rove
And coy bumbarrels twenty in a drove
Flit down the hedgerows in the frozen plain
And hang on little twigs and start again

JOHN CLARE (1793–1864)

awe: haw   *bumbarrels:* long-tailed tits   *closen:* small enclosed fields

The Lake Isle of Innisfree

I will arise and go now, and go to Innisfree,
And a small cabin build there, of clay and wattles made:
Nine bean-rows will I have there, a hive for the honey-bee,
And live alone in the bee-loud glade.

And I shall have some peace there, for peace comes
    dropping slow,
Dropping from the veils of the morning to where the
    cricket sings;
There midnight's all a glimmer, and noon a purple glow,
And evening full of the linnet's wings.

I will arise and go now, for always night and day
I hear lake water lapping with low sounds by the shore;
While I stand on the roadway, or on the pavements grey,
I hear it in the deep heart's core.

W. B. YEATS (1865–1939)

I May, I Might, I Must

If you will tell me why the fen
appears impassable, I then
will tell you why I think that I
can get across it if I try.

MARIANNE MOORE (1887–1972)

Separation

Your absence has gone through me
Like thread through a needle.
Everything I do is stitched with its colour.

W. S. MERWIN (b. 1927)

N.W.2: Spring

The poets never lied when they praised
Spring in England.
                  Even in this neat suburb
You can feel there's something to
                            their pastorals.
Something gentle, broadly nostalgic, is stirring
On the well-aired pavements.
                      Indrawn brick
Sighs, and you notice the sudden sharpness
Of things growing.
                The sun lightens
The significance of what the houses
Are steeped in,
             brightens out
Their winter brooding.
              Early May
Touches also the cold diasporas
That England hardly mentions.

A. C. JACOBS (1937–94)

Roundel

Since I from Love escaped am so fat,
I never think to be in his prison lean;
Since I am free, I count him not a bean.

He may answer and say right this and that;
I do no force, I speak right as I mean.
  Since I from Love escaped am so fat,
  I never think to be in his prison lean.

Love hath my name stricken out of his slate,
And he is struck out of my bookés clean
For ever more, there is no other mean.
  Since I from Love escaped am so fat,
  I never think to be in his prison lean;
  Since I am free, I count him not a bean.

GEOFFREY CHAUCER (1340?–1400)

I do no force: I care not

'Since I from Love escaped am so fat' MS Pepys 2006, p.391, reprinted by permission of the Pepys Library, Magdalene College Cambridge.

'I saw a man pursuing the horizon'

I saw a man pursuing the horizon;
Round and round they sped.
I was disturbed at this;
I accosted the man.
"It is futile," I said,
"You can never—"

"You lie," he cried,
And ran on.

STEPHEN CRANE (1871–1900)

Cut Grass

Cut grass lies frail:
Brief is the breath
Mown stalks exhale.
Long, long the death

It dies in the white hours
Of young-leafed June
With chestnut flowers,
With hedges snowlike strewn,

White lilac bowed,
Lost lanes of Queen Anne's lace,
And that high-builded cloud
Moving at summer's pace.

PHILIP LARKIN (1922–85)

The Two Apes of Brueghel

Here's my dream of a final exam:
two apes, in chains, sitting at a window.
Outside the sky is flying
and the sea bathes.

I am taking the test on human history.
I stammer and blunder.

One ape, staring at me, listens with irony,
the other seems to doze –
but when I am silent after a question,
she prompts me
with a soft clanking of the chain.

WISŁAWA SZYMBORSKA (b. 1923)
translated by GRAZYNA DRABIK *with* SHARON OLDS

Once

after 'Ya Vas Liubil' by Alexander Pushkin

I loved you once. D'you hear a small '*I love you*'
  Each time we're forced to meet? Don't groan, don't hide!
A damaged tree can live without a bud:
  No one need break the branches and uncover
The green that should have danced, dying inside.
  I loved you, knowing I'd never be your lover.
And now? I wish you summers of leaf-shine
  And leaf-shade, and a face in dreams above you,
  As tender and as innocent as mine.

CAROL RUMENS (b. 1944)

Web

The deftest leave no trace: type, send, delete,
clear *history*. The world will never know.
Though a man might wonder, as he crossed the street
what it was that broke across his brow
or vanished on his tongue and left it sweet

DON PATERSON (b. 1963)

The Long War

Less passionate the long war throws
its burning thorn about all men,
caught in one grief, we share one wound,
and cry one dialect of pain.

We have forgot who fired the house,
whose easy mischief spilt first blood,
under one raging roof we lie
the fault no longer understood.

But as our twisted arms embrace
the desert where our cities stood,
death's family likeness in each face
must show, at last, our brotherhood.

LAURIE LEE (1914–97)

'Autumn evening'

Autumn evening –
A crow on a bare branch.

MATSUO BASHŌ (1644–94)
translated by KENNETH REXROTH

'Autumn evening' Calligraphy by Yukki Yaura,
specially commissioned from the artist by Poems
on the Underground. © Yukki Yaura 2004.

う枯枝に鳥の
止り
秋の暮

芭蕉

On Lake Nicaragua

Slow cargo-launch, midnight, mid-lake,
bound from San Miguelito to Granada.
The lights ahead not yet in sight,
the dwindling ones behind completely gone.
Only the stars
(the mast a finger pointing to the Seven Sisters)
                and the moon, rising above Chontales.

Another launch (just one red light) goes by
and sinks into the night.
We, for them:
             another red light sinking in the night...
And I, watching the stars, lying on the deck
between bunches of bananas and Chontales cheeses,
wonder: perhaps there's one that is an earth like ours
and someone's watching me (watching the stars)
from another launch, on another night, on another lake.

ERNESTO CARDENAL (b. 1925)

translated by ERNESTO CARDENAL *and* ROBERT PRING-MILL

Poem on the Underground

Proud readers
Hide behind tall newspapers.

The young are all arms and legs
Knackered by youth.

Tourists sit bolt upright
Trusting in nothing.

Only the drunk and the crazy
Aspire to converse.

Only the poet
Peruses his poem among the adverts.

Only the elderly person
Observes the request that the seat be offered to an
    elderly person.

D. J. ENRIGHT (1920–2002)

Anti-Slavery Movements

Some people say
Animal liberators are not
Working in the interest of animals.
But I've never seen liberated animals
Protest by going back to their place
Of captivity.
But then again
I've never heard of any liberated slaves
Begging for more humiliation
Or voting for slavery.

Animals vote with their feet
Or their wings
Or their fins.

BENJAMIN ZEPHANIAH (b. 1958)

Content

Like walking in fog, in fog and mud,
do you remember, love? We kept,
for once, to the tourist path, boxed in mist,
conscious of just our feet and breath,
and at the peak, sat hand in hand, and let
the cliffs we'd climbed and cliffs to come
reveal themselves and be veiled again
quietly, with the prevailing wind.

KATE CLANCHY (b. 1965)

Rhapsody

Sat in the cheap seats
Of Symphony Hall, squinting
As the instruments tuned up
I could pick out only you:
Fourth row back and clutching
Your viola, bright hair spilt
Across the strings. You were
Deep in a flurry of pages
With bitten lip, too
Intent on forcing that
Melody right to the cheap seats
To notice me up there, ears straining
To block out any sound but yours.

BEN ZIMAN-BRIGHT

Stitching the Bayeux Tapestry

First of all I learn to sheathe my mind
in a needle, a shining domestic
wand with a steely eye and a
sharp bite. Hovering over the battlefield
like a hand-held bird of prey, it darts and
dips its nimble beak into the freshly spilled
colour, dining off a raw pink and grey
palate of corpses and savouring
the acrid metal stench of victory. I sew
the winner's story, embroidering detail and carefully
twisting fact. Beneath my guilty fingertips
the tapestry seems to bulge and tighten,
throttling the truth with its linen coils.

REBECCA HAWKES

Pigeon Patterns

On the steps they are building a life out of crumbs,
Little piles of our discarded food turned to monuments.
Around the Starbucks morning stall, with its electric hums,
They gather us up, to herd us in some absurd grey waltz.

They seem so trite, so decadent,
Clutched like aristocrats with one good, faded coat
Scrounging beneath banks and out-door restaurants.
We raise a shoe to feather the air. Dust particles, like
    dollars, float.

When you think about it, maybe we would do better
To make a ceremony out of ordinary acts, to tap everyday
    trails.
Catching the train would be much more exciting if we all
    spread
Our smiles as pigeons wave their ice-cream wafer tails.
    Those pointless bills.

L. E. HARRIS

To Althea, from Prison

When Love with unconfined wings
   Hovers within my gates,
And my divine Althea brings
   To whisper at the grates;
When I lie tangled in her hair
   And fettered to her eye,
The gods that wanton in the air
   Know no such liberty...

Stone walls do not a prison make,
   Nor iron bars a cage;
Minds innocent and quiet take
   That for an hermitage.
If I have freedom in my love,
   And in my soul am free,
Angels alone, that soar above,
   Enjoy such liberty.

lines 1–8, 25–32

RICHARD LOVELACE (1618–57)

Heredity

I am the family face;
Flesh perishes, I live on,
Projecting trait and trace
Through time to times anon,
And leaping from place to place
Over oblivion.

The years-heired feature that can
In curve and voice and eye
Despise the human span
Of durance – that is I;
The eternal thing in man,
That heeds no call to die.

THOMAS HARDY (1840–1928)

First Book of Odes (6)

... As to my heart, that may as well be forgotten
or labelled: Owner will dispose of same
to a good home, refs. exchgd., h.&c.,
previous experience desired but not essential
or let on a short lease to suit convenience.

BASIL BUNTING (1900–85)

Belgrade

White bone among the clouds

You arise out of your pyre
Out of your ploughed-up barrows
Out of your scattered ashes

You arise out of your disappearance

The sun keeps you
In its golden reliquary
High above the yapping of centuries

And bears you to the marriage
Of the fourth river of Paradise
With the thirty-sixth river of Earth

White bone among the clouds
Bone of our bones

VASKO POPA (1922–91)
translated from the Serbo-Croat by ANNE PENNINGTON

Coltsfoot and Larches

I love coltsfoot that they
Make their appearance into life among dead grass:
Larches, that they
Die colourfully among sombre immortals.

DAVID CONSTANTINE (b. 1944)

The Creel

The world began with a woman,
shawl-happed, stooped under a creel,
whose slow step you recognize
from troubled dreams. You feel

obliged to help bear her burden
from hill or kelp-strewn shore,
but she passes by unseeing
thirled to her private chore.

It's not sea birds or peat she's carrying,
not fleece, nor the herring bright
but her fear that if ever she put it down
the world would go out like a light.

KATHLEEN JAMIE (b. 1962)

creel: wicker basket for carrying fish, peat, etc on the back
thirled: enslaved

from **Doctor Faustus**

Was this the face that launched a thousand ships
And burnt the topless towers of Ilium?
Sweet Helen, make me immortal with a kiss.
Her lips suck forth my soul – see where it flies!
Come, Helen, come, give me my soul again.
Here will I dwell, for heaven is in these lips,
And all is dross that is not Helena...

O, thou art fairer than the evening air
Clad in the beauty of a thousand stars!
Brighter art thou than flaming Jupiter
When he appeared to hapless Semele,
More lovely than the monarch of the sky
In wanton Arethusa's azured arms,
And none but thou shalt be my paramour!

Act V. i. 99–105, 112–18

CHRISTOPHER MARLOWE (1564–93)

'I stepped from Plank to Plank'

I stepped from Plank to Plank
A slow and cautious way
The Stars about my Head I felt
About my Feet the Sea.

I knew not but the next
Would be my final inch –
This gave me that precarious Gait
Some call Experience.

EMILY DICKINSON (1830–86)

'When I was one-and-twenty'

When I was one-and-twenty
  I heard a wise man say,
"Give crowns and pounds and guineas
  But not your heart away;
Give pearls away and rubies
  But keep your fancy free."
But I was one-and-twenty,
  No use to talk to me.

When I was one-and-twenty
  I heard him say again,
"The heart out of the bosom
  Was never given in vain;
'Tis paid with sighs a plenty
  And sold for endless rue."
And I am two-and-twenty,
  And oh, 'tis true, 'tis true.

A. E. HOUSMAN (1859–1936)

Animals

Have you forgotten what we were like then
when we were still first rate
and the day came fat with an apple in its mouth

it's no use worrying about Time
but we did have a few tricks up our sleeves
and turned some sharp corners

the whole pasture looked like our meal
we didn't need speedometers
we could manage cocktails out of ice and water

I wouldn't want to be faster
or greener than now if you were with me O you
were the best of all my days

FRANK O'HARA (1926–66)

Tides

There are some coasts
Where the sea comes in spectacularly
Throwing itself up gullies, challenging cliffs,
Filling the harbours with great swirls and flourish,
A theatrical event that people gather for
Curtain up twice daily. You need to know
The hour of its starting, you have to be on guard.

There are other places
Places where you do not really notice
The gradual stretch of the fertile silk of water
No gurgling or dashings here, no froth no pounding
Only at some point the echo may sound different
And looking by chance one sees 'Oh the tide is in.'

JENNY JOSEPH (b. 1932)

Canticle

Sometimes when you walk down to the red gate
hearing the scrape-music of your shoes across gravel,
a yellow moon will lift over the hill;
you swing the gate shut and lean on the topmost bar
as if something has been accomplished in the world;
a night wind mistles through the poplar leaves
and all the noise of the universe stills
to an oboe hum, the given note of a perfect
music; there is a vast sky wholly dedicated
to the stars and you know, with certainty,
that all the dead are out, up there, in one
holiday flotilla, and that they celebrate
the fact of a red gate and a yellow moon
that tunes their instruments with you to the symphony.

JOHN F. DEANE (b. 1943)

David's lament for Jonathan

How are the mighty fallen in the midst of the battle!
O Jonathan, thou wast slain in thine high places.

I am distressed for thee, my brother Jonathan:
   very pleasant hast thou been unto me:
    thy love to me was wonderful, passing the love of women.

How are the mighty fallen, and the weapons of war perished!

II Samuel 1: 25–27

THE KING JAMES BIBLE (1611)

from Ode: Intimations of Immortality

There was a time when meadow, grove, and stream,
The earth, and every common sight,
  To me did seem
  Apparell'd in celestial light,
The glory and the freshness of a dream.
It is not now as it hath been of yore; –
  Turn wheresoe'er I may,
   By night or day,
The things which I have seen I now can see no more.

  The Rainbow comes and goes,
  And lovely is the Rose,
  The Moon doth with delight
Look round her when the heavens are bare;
  Waters on a starry night
  Are beautiful and fair;
 The sunshine is a glorious birth;
 But yet I know, where'er I go,
That there hath pass'd away a glory from the earth.

lines 1–18

WILLIAM WORDSWORTH (1770–1850)

Words in Time

Bewildered with the broken tongue
Of wakened angels in our sleep –
Then, lost the music that was sung
And lost the light time cannot keep!

There is a moment when we lie
Bewildered, wakened out of sleep,
When light and sound and all reply:
That moment time must tame and keep.

That moment, like a flight of birds
Flung from the branches where they sleep,
The poet with a beat of words
Flings into time for time to keep.

ARCHIBALD MacLEISH (1892–1982)

One Perfect Rose

A single flow'r he sent me, since we met.
   All tenderly his messenger he chose;
Deep-hearted, pure, with scented dew still wet –
   One perfect rose.

I knew the language of the floweret;
   "My fragile leaves," it said, "his heart enclose."
Love long has taken for his amulet
   One perfect rose.

Why is it no one ever sent me yet
   One perfect limousine, do you suppose?
Ah no, it's always just my luck to get
   One perfect rose.

DOROTHY PARKER (1893–1967)

If Bach Had Been a Beekeeper

for Arvo Pärt

If Bach had been a beekeeper
he would have heard
all those notes
suspended above one another
in the air of his ear
as the differentiated swarm returning
to the exact hive
and place in the hive,
topping up the cells
with the honey of C major,
food for the listening generations,
key to their comfort
and solace of their distress
as they return and return
to those counterpointed levels
of hovering wings where
movement is dance
and the air itself
a scented garden

CHARLES TOMLINSON (b. 1927)

My children

I can hear them talking, my children
fluent English and broken Kurdish.

And whenever I disagree with them
they will comfort each other by saying:
Don't worry about mum, she's Kurdish.

Will I be the foreigner in my own home?

CHOMAN HARDI (b. 1974)

Listening to a Monk from Shu Playing the Lute

The monk from Shu with his green lute-case walked
Westward down Emei Shan, and at the sound
Of the first notes he strummed for me I heard
A thousand valleys' rustling pines resound.
My heart was cleansed, as if in flowing water.
In bells of frost I heard the resonance die.
Dusk came unnoticed over the emerald hills
And autumn clouds layered the darkening sky.

LI BAI (AD 701–61)
translated by VIKRAM SETH

Calligraphy by Qu Lei Lei

The Beautiful Toilet

Blue, blue is the grass about the river
And the willows have overfilled the close garden.
And within, the mistress, in the midmost of her youth,
White, white of face, hesitates, passing the door.
Slender, she puts forth a slender hand;

And she was a courtesan in the old days,
And she has married a sot,
Who now goes drunkenly out
And leaves her too much alone.

ANON. (1st century AD)
translated by EZRA POUND

Calligraphy by Qu Lei Lei

青之河

畔艸

The Red Cockatoo

Sent as a present from Annam –
A red cockatoo.
Coloured like the peach-tree blossom,
Speaking with the speech of men.

And they did to it what is always done
To the learned and eloquent.
They took a cage with stout bars
And shut it up inside.

PO CHU-I (AD 772–846)

translated by ARTHUR WALEY

New Year 1933

The general sits safe on his cloud-wrapped peak
While thunderbolts slaughter the humble in their hovels.
Far better to live in the International Settlement,
Where the clacking of mahjong heralds the spring.

LU XUN (1881–1936)
translated by W. J. F. JENNER

Calligraphy by Qu Lei Lei

'When I have fears that I may cease to be'

When I have fears that I may cease to be
  Before my pen has glean'd my teeming brain,
Before high-piled books, in charact'ry,
  Hold like rich garners the full-ripen'd grain;
When I behold, upon the night's starr'd face,
  Huge cloudy symbols of a high romance,
And think that I may never live to trace
  Their shadows, with the magic hand of chance;
And when I feel, fair creature of an hour!
  That I shall never look upon thee more,
Never have relish in the faery power
  Of unreflecting love! – then on the shore
Of the wide world I stand alone, and think
Till love and fame to nothingness do sink.

JOHN KEATS (1795–1821)

'There was an Old Man of Blackheath'

There was an Old Man of Blackheath,
Whose head was adorned with a Wreath,
    Of lobsters and spice,
    Pickled onions and mice,
That uncommon Old Man of Blackheath.

EDWARD LEAR (1812–88)

'There was an Old Man of Blackheath' Drawing
by the author, from *The Book of Nonsense*.

Birch Canoe

Red men embraced   my body's whiteness,
cutting into me   carved it free,
sewed it tight   with sinews taken
from lightfoot deer   who leaped this stream –
now in my ghost-skin   they glide over clouds
at home in the fish's   fallen heaven.

CARTER REVARD (b. 1931)

Promise

Remember, the time of year
when the future appears
like a blank sheet of paper
a clean calendar, a new chance.
On thick white snow

you vow fresh footprints
then watch them go
with the wind's hearty gust.
Fill your glass. Here's tae us. Promises
made to be broken, made to last.

JACKIE KAY (b. 1961)

NOTES TO THE POEMS

18 **The Ancient Mariner** These stanzas, coming half-way through Coleridge's famous ballad, mark the turning point in the Mariner's fearful tale of guilt and punishment. The poem began as a light-hearted collaboration between Coleridge and Wordsworth, meant to defray expenses for a walking tour in the Quantocks. The resulting ballad, incorporating a few key suggestions by Wordsworth and allusions to Coleridge's vast readings in explorers' narratives and anti-slavery tracts, was first published anonymously in *Lyrical Ballads* (1798). Since that time, 'The Ancient Mariner' has inspired more critical commentary than any other work in English, with the possible exception of *Hamlet*. (The curious reader is referred to "The Mariner, the Flying Dutchman, and the Wandering Jew" by J.C. in *TLS*, 24 January 2003.)

21 **Should You Die First** Annabelle Despard is a bilingual poet who writes in Norwegian and makes her own translations into English. In 1998, when two of our editors took up a six-week writers' residency in Stavanger and Kristiansand, supported by the British Council, Annabelle provided valuable advice on how to identify the difference between the poisonous and the edible fungi which grew in the surrounding countryside. The original Norwegian text of 'Should You Die First' was published in *Bolgende lang som Amerika* (Aschehoug); the Tube poster marked the first publication of the English text.

23 **Commonwealth Poems on the Underground** In celebration of the half-century since the founding of the Commonwealth, the Foreign & Commonwealth Office invited us to produce a series of poems by poets born in the Commonwealth, now numbering fifty-

seven countries. We selected 20th-century poets representing Canada (Earle Birney), New Zealand (Lauris Edmond), Nigeria (J.P. Clark-Bekederemo), India (Dom Moraes), Milawi (Jack Mapanje), Trinidad (Faustin Charles), Jamaica (Merle Collins) and Pakistan (Moniza Alvi). (Of these poets, only the first three lived mainly in their country of birth.) 'Viv' by Faustin Charles and 'Indian Cooking' by Moniza Alvi were distributed to 34,000 schools as part of National Poetry Day.

23 **giovanni caboto/john cabot** Born in Genoa c.1450, Giovanni Caboto moved to Venice, becoming a mapmaker and trader. Convinced that the great riches of Asia could be reached by going west, Caboto, soon to become 'John Cabot,' moved to Bristol, which was fast becoming the chief port for voyages across the Atlantic. In 1496, King Henry VII financed Cabot's first voyage in search of a north-west passage, the condition being that Cabot should give the king one-fifth of any profits. The voyagers found vast shoals of cod near Cape Breton, Nova Scotia, where they landed, and little else. On his return Cabot reported that he had reached the country of the Grand Khan, where silk and brazilwood could be purchased, and he proposed a second voyage to Cipango, as Japan was then known. During his second trip to North America in 1498, Cabot ran into violent storms and was presumed to have drowned.

The Canadian poet Earle Birney lived for extended periods in France and Mexico. In 1934, he worked his passage to England on a tramp freighter, later visiting Trotsky in Norway. In Berlin, Birney was arrested by the Gestapo for refusing to salute a Nazi parade. After his return home, he became an inspirational teacher, writing many volumes of poetry, plays and novels.

25 **Ibadan** Nigeria's second largest city, and home of a major university, Ibadan is built on seven hills, and its dry, mineral-rich soil is rust-coloured (described memorably in Wole Soyinka's auto-biography *Ibadan*).

27 **The Palm Trees at Chigawe** Shortly after its publication in 1986, *Of Chameleons and Gods* was banned and its author arrested by the Malawi authorities. Jack Mapanje was imprisoned from 1987 to 1991, detained without charge or trial. He has lived since 1991 in Britain.

28 **Viv** Vivian Richards captained the West Indian cricket team during the 1980s. He was an imperious and aggressive batsman with a superb technique, in command of all the shots. He was the 20th-century player who more than any other dominated and demoralised opposing bowlers. By birth he was an Antiguan, proud of his ancestry. His demeanour on and off the pitch was much the same, self-confident to the point of arrogance; he was a fierce and outspoken opponent of racism in sport and in the outside world. He was a close friend of his Somerset team-mate, Ian Botham. Together they provided inspiring role models for a generation.

31 **A Tune** A sentiment echoed by Amanda in Noel Coward's *Private Lives*: "Extraordinary how potent cheap music is."

33 **Fine Knacks for Ladies** A pedlar's song. The travelling pedlar with his tray of cheap merchandise was a common figure at medieval and Tudor fairs. These travellers usually sang the penny ballads they were selling, rather than highly wrought lyrics such as 'Fine Knacks for Ladies,' elegantly set by the court composer John Dowland. 'Orient' in this context means 'shining'; 'turtle' is a dove; 'remove' is the transference of affections, as in Shakespeare's Sonnet 116: "Love is not love that alters when it alteration finds / Or bends with the remover to remove." Dowland's setting is still popular with choirs, glee clubs and madrigal groups.

34 **Sonnet on Chillon** This is one of several poems composed during the famous 'Geneva summer' of 1816, when Byron lived with his entourage in the Villa Diodati, on the shores of Lake Geneva;

Shelley, Mary Shelley and Claire Clairmont took a more modest house a few hundred yards away. The visiting back and forth had a powerful impact on both poets; and Byron's suggestion, during a prolonged rainy spell, that they each begin a vampire tale, inspired Mary Shelley's *Frankenstein*. In July the two poets took a boat round the lake, stopping at sites associated with Rousseau, Voltaire and Gibbon. At the castle of Chillon they heard the sad tale of the political prisoner Bonnivard (1496–1570). Byron's sonnet, with its stirring opening lines, introduces 'The Prisoner of Chillon', which recounts the full story.

36 **Accordionist** George Szirtes was born in Budapest, and came to Britain as a refugee in 1956, having walked with his parents and younger brother into Austria, where they remained in a refugee camp until a flight to Britain was arranged.

39 **August 1914** Isaac Rosenberg, the son of Russian Jewish émigrés, was educated at council schools in London's east end. He was bitterly opposed to the First World War, and was convinced of its futility. Unable to earn his living as a poet or an artist (he had been trained at the Slade), he enlisted for the sake of the modest pay of a private, which he hoped would relieve the poverty of his family. He was killed in action, aged 28, on 1 April 1918.

40 **Young Poets on the Underground** This was our second display of poems by entrants in the Poetry Society's annual competition for young poets. Winners and runners-up were invited to submit short poems suitable for display on the Tube, and we selected three entries for display.

43 **European Poems on the Underground** To mark Britain's thirty years in the EU (1973-2003), the Foreign & Commonwealth Office invited us to display poems in bilingual texts from nine of the fifteen EU member states. The selection of poems was informally

linked to bilingual poetry displays in Paris and Stuttgart; both cities have offered poems on public transport for several years, in programmes originally inspired by London's Poems on the Underground. Adrian Mitchell's two-line poem 'Goodbye', in homage to the jazz saxophonist Charlie Parker, was featured on the Paris Metro; and Stuttgart included 'Music, when soft voices die,' by Shelley. Our own 'European Poems' were launched at Westminster Underground by Denis MacShane, at that time Minister for Europe, followed by a grand reception at the India Room in the Foreign Office.

43 **Inferno** The Irish Nobel prizewinner's translation of Dante's *Inferno*, Canto 1, seemed an appropriate introduction to our European series, otherwise devoted to 20th-century poets.

44 **'The waves, blue walls'** Rafael Alberti fought for the Republic in the Spanish Civil War and fled to Argentina after the Fascists took power. He moved to Italy in 1961 and returned to Spain after Franco's defeat in 1977. *Marinero en Tierra* (1925) was his first publication, and includes many illustrations inspired by Alberti's native Cadiz.

46 **Miracle** Like Alberti, Yannis Ritsos was a socialist, joining the Greek Communist Party as a young man. He was imprisoned repeatedly for his political beliefs, and exiled to various Greek islands from 1948 to 1952, and between 1967 and 1971. He remained amazingly prolific, and several of his poems were set to music by Mikis Theodorakis and other popular Greek composers.

47 **In the Poem** As part of the launch of the Porto Metro, 'No poema' was displayed in Portuguese and English, along with an English poem from our collection ('Words Wide Night' by Carol Ann Duffy).

56 **Homage to the British Museum** William Empson's tribute to the Museum and one of its more unusual objects, a statue of the Polynesian god A'a, was the centre-piece of a reading we gave in the Reading Room as part of the Museum's 250th-anniversary celebrations. We commissioned Laurie Lipton's drawing specially for *New Poems*.

59 **Poetry** Saadi Youssef, born in Basra, has lived in exile from Iraq for many years, and now lives in London. He joined us for our reading at the British Museum, which took place just after the Museum in Baghdad had been severely looted.

60 **The London Eye** In 2002, Shakespeare's Globe Theatre, in collaboration with the Wordsworth Trust, commissioned 37 poets to write sonnets in response to Wordsworth's sonnet, "Composed Upon Westminster Bridge, September 3, 1802." The resulting volume, *Earth has not any thing to shew more fair*, published to mark the bicentenary of the original sonnet, contains Patience Agbabi's 'The London Eye'– a modern take on the sonnet's perennial theme of Time. Wordsworth's sonnet appears in the 10th Edition of *Poems on the Underground*.

63 **I have a young sister** This text, the earliest known version of the song popularised as 'I gave my love a cherry', appears in the same 15th-century manuscript collection as 'I have a gentil cock' and 'I sing of a maiden', both in our 10th Edition. Alternative versions of the song have been recorded in many far-flung places, including Somerset and the Appalachian hills.

64 **Infant Joy** Blake conceived of his *Songs of Innocence and of Experience* as complementary sequences. Paired with 'Infant Joy', from *Songs of Innocence*, is 'Infant Sorrow,' from *Songs of Experience:*

> My mother groaned! my father wept,
> Into the dangerous world I leapt:

Helpless, naked, piping loud:
Like a fiend hid in a cloud.

Struggling in my father's hands:
Striving against my swaddling bands:
Bound and weary I thought best
To sulk upon my mother's breast.

We would have liked to display both poems on the Tube, but felt that 'Infant Joy' offered a more positive message to weary commuters. The British Museum owns several copies of the *Songs*, hand-coloured by Blake and his wife Catherine. As 'Infant Joy' circulated on the Tube, we were delighted to offer a reading of the complete *Songs* in the Reading Room, with slides of the original images, and Vaughan Williams' settings for oboe and voice (arranged for oboe and cello).

65 **Dream** Kathleen Raine, who died in 2003 at the age of 95, was a follower of Blake, by whom she was profoundly influenced, and on whose work she was a leading authority. In her later years, she founded the Temenos Academy near Regents Park, which was to be a new 'school of wisdom'. Kathleen Raine spent her early childhood in Northumbria and the beauty of its wild countryside remained an inspiration throughout her life.

66 **Exodus** Lotte Kramer, born in Mainz, Germany, came to England as a child refugee in 1939 on the Kindertransport.

67 **The bee dance** Ken Smith was poet-in-residence at Wormwood Scrubs prison, and the poems in *Wormwood*, including 'The bee dance', often represent the experiences of the prisoners incarcerated there. Born in Yorkshire, the son of an itinerant farm labourer, Ken Smith worked in Britain and America as a teacher, barman, magazine editor, potato picker and BBC reader. His poems reflect his lifelong commitment to social justice.

70 **The Lake Isle of Innisfree** In his autobiography, W. B.Yeats wrote: "... when walking through Fleet Street very homesick I heard a little tinkle of water and saw a fountain in a shop-window which balanced a little ball upon its jet, and began to remember lake water. From my sudden remembrance came my poem Innisfree, my first lyric with anything in its rhythm of my own music." In later years Yeats was to complain that he was obliged to include Innisfree in all his readings, since it was the one poem of his that was universally known. As a young man who had read Thoreau's essays, he had wanted to live in peace in a hut on the isle of Innisfree, on Loch Gill. In a BBC programme (one of the few remaining recordings of Yeats reading), he said of the poem: "I speak of the purple glow. I must have meant, I think, the reflection of heather in the water." Innisfree means 'heather island'.

73 **N.W. 2: Spring** Arthur Jacobs was a distinguished translator of Hebrew poetry as well as a lyric poet in his own right. Born in Glasgow, he grew up in a traditional Jewish family, attended the Hasmonean Grammar School in London, and lived in Spain, Israel, Scotland and Italy as well as Hendon, north London, a pleasant suburb closely observed in 'N.W.2: Spring.'

74 **Roundel** One of three 'roundels' collectively entitled "Merciles Beaute", attributed to Chaucer in Pepys 2006, a 15th-century manuscript collection of Chaucer's works. The attribution to Chaucer has been questioned, but the colloquial language and self-mockery are consistent with the 'simple' narrator of the Canterbury Tales, as described by the Host in the prologue to Chaucer's *Tale of Sir Thopas*:

> He in the waist is shape(d) as well as I
> This were a poppet in an arm t'embrace
> For any woman, small and fair of face...

76 **'I saw a man pursuing the horizon'** The American poet Stephen Crane was the son of parents who were militant leaders in the Methodist movement. He published *The Black Riders,* his first book of poems, in 1895, shortly after completing his anti-war novel about the American Civil War, *The Red Badge of Courage.* Most of the poems in *The Black Riders* reflect his fierce rebellion against his parents' religion. The first edition was printed in capital letters throughout, an innovation we followed in the Tube poster.

78 **The Two Apes of Brueghel** Wisława Szymborska, one of Poland's most distinguished contemporary poets, was awarded the Nobel Prize for Literature in 1996. In an introduction to her *Selected Poems,* Czeslaw Milosz (also a Nobel prizewinner) wrote: "Szymborska brings joy because she is so sharp, because she derives pleasure out of juggling the props of our common heritage, and because she has such a good sense of the comic...[Her] playfulness gives us, in spite of everything else, a feeling for the enormous diversity and splendour of human existence."

79 **Once** One of several "Rogue Translations" by Carol Rumens inspired by Pushkin, Anna Akhmatova, Osip Mandelstam and Ovid. 'Once' may also remind readers of Tatiana's doomed love for Eugene Onegin, in Pushkin's famous 'novel in verse'.

81 **The Long War** Laurie Lee first visited Spain in 1936 at the time of the Spanish Civil War. His much-loved book, *Cider with Rosie,* tells the story of his early life as one of a family of eight children living in a small Gloucestershire cottage.

82 **'Autumn evening'** Matsuo Kinsaku, a Buddhist monk, was one of the earliest and greatest haiku poets. He changed his name to Bashō in honour of a present of a basho tree, known for its broad leaves, sensitive to the least wind. "In this poor body," he wrote, "composed of one hundred bones and nine openings, is some-

thing called a spirit, a flimsy curtain swept this way and that by the slightest breeze. It is this spirit, such as it is, which led me to poetry." He was particularly attracted to the haiku form and wrote more than a thousand examples. As an antidote to superficiality he recommended a lightness of touch: ".. a good poem is one in which the form of the verse and the joining of its ... parts seem light as a shallow river flowing over its sandy bed."

84 **On Lake Nicaragua** Born in the town of Granada, Nicaragua, Cardenal studied at the Universities of Mexico and Columbia. In 1956 he entered the Trappist Monastery in Kentucky where he studied with Thomas Merton, who was to be a profound influence on his life and writing. Cardenal was ordained at the age of 40 and set up a religious commune in Solentiname on Lake Nicaragua. After the Sandinista revolution of 1978, when the dictator was overthrown, Cardenal became Nicaragua's first Minister of Culture and instituted a national literacy programme. Poetry became a passion and language of the people.

88 **Young Poets on the Underground** Our third competition in association with the Poetry Society. See Note 40 above.

91 **To Althea, from Prison** Richard Lovelace, the heir to great estates in Kent, served in the court of Charles I and was imprisoned for presenting the Kentish petition in favour of the King in 1642. (This is the period to which 'To Althea, from Prison' refers). He later fought abroad, and was imprisoned again on his return to England in 1648. On his release, now penniless, a contemporary described him as growing 'very melancholy; [he] became very poor in body and person, was the object of charity, went in ragged cloathes (whereas when he was in his glory he wore cloth of gold and silver) and mostly lodged in obscure and dirty places, more befitting the worst of beggars and poorest of servants.' He is remembered as a leading 'Cavalier' poet, one of the 'sons of Ben [Jonson]', classically trained and Royalist in their sympathies.

---

94 **Belgrade** The city of Belgrade, standing as it does between the east and the west, has withstood many attacks in its long history. In the early 1970s, when Vasko Popa was writing the long cycle 'Earth Erect', in which 'Belgrade' is the final poem, the most recent attack had been the Nazi Luftwaffe raid in April 1941. But perhaps no onslaught has caused its people more distress and anger than the bombing of the city by NATO forces in 1999.

'Earth Erect' tells of St Sava, the patron saint of Serbia, and his healing springs. Here the legendary St Sava is portrayed as an old man, a shepherd who tends his flock of wolves – traditionally the Serb people. In the fifth and final cycle the traveller returns to 'The White City', where the river Sava meets the Danube, 'the fourth river of paradise.'

Historically, St Sava was a dynastic prince, born in 1175, who became a monk on Mount Athos and later built the famous monastery of Hilandar. St Sava created the Serbian church and state, bringing culture and learning to his people. By the four-teenth century, as a result of his inspirational teachings, Serbia had become the foremost nation in the Balkans.

95 **Coltsfoot and Larches** Another short poem on the same theme, 'Coltsfoot', beautifully evokes the poet's childhood:

> Coming before my birthday they are for ever your flowers
> Who are dead and at whose hand
> I picked them on the allotments and blitzed land.

97 *from* **Doctor Faustus** Since he made a pact with the devil, Faustus has acquired supernatural powers. In this passage Faustus greets the greatest beauty of the classical world: Helen of Troy, conjured for Faustus by Mephistophilis, servant to Lucifer. The classical allusions contain subliminal warnings: Semele desired Jupiter to appear before her in his full glory as a god, but when he did, she was destroyed by the lightning which always accompanied him.

The nymph Arethusa was transformed into a fountain; thus Helen is lovelier than sunlight reflected in the water, but, alas, the beauty of sunlight on a fountain is insubstantial.

99 **'When I was one-and-twenty'** Our long-suffering and loyal editor, Barry Holmes, told us that this is his favourite poem. 'It should be memorised by all young men,' he told us – though, he added, his wife might disagree.

104 **Ode: Intimations of Immortality** Full title: 'Ode: Intimations of Immortality from Recollections of Early Childhood', (first two stanzas). Wordsworth traced the poem's roots to his sense in childhood 'of the indomitableness of the spirit within me'. These stanzas were written on 27 March 1802, when his sister Dorothy noted in her Journal: 'A divine morning – at Breakfast Wm wrote part of an ode – Mr Olliff sent the Dung & Wm went to work in the garden we sate all day in the Orchard.'

105 **Words in Time** Three times a Pulitzer Prize winner, Archibald MacLeish was a poet, a playwright, a lawyer, a teacher, Librarian of Congress, Assistant Secretary of State under President Roosevelt. A constant proponent of human liberty, he was called a fascist by communists and a communist by Senator Joseph McCarthy. He opposed the Vietnam war and years before that was a scathing and perceptive critic of society. He published over forty books of poems, and is probably best known for his poem 'Ars Poetica' in which he says, enigmatically: 'A poem should not mean/ But be.'

108 **My children** Choman Hardi was born in southern Kurdistan, now part of Iraq. Her father, Ahmad Hardi, a highly regarded Kurdish poet, instilled in his daughter a love of their language. When Choman Hardi was still very young, her family was exiled and went to live in Iran, coming home again after five years. In

1988, after the Kurds were attacked by the chemical weapons launched by their own government, the family once again fled their homeland. Choman Hardi came to England in 1993 to study philosophy and psychology at Oxford and later obtained an MA in philosophy at University College, London. She now writes her poems in English, the language of her adopted country and of her children.

109 Chinese Poems on the Underground In 2005, the British Council in Shanghai, on behalf of Shanghai Metro, proposed that we organise an exchange of poems, featuring Chinese poems in London and British poems in Shanghai. We agreed to display poems drawn from two thousand years of Chinese poetry, one from the Han dynasty (first century AD), two from the great Tang period (AD 618–906), and one from the early twentieth century. All four posters in our display included specially commissioned calligraphy by Qu Lei Lei, a leading calligrapher and painter who moved to London in 1985; in China he was a founding member of the Stars Art Movement, which fought for artistic freedom of expression after the Cultural Revolution.

109 **Listening to a Monk from Shu Playing the Lute** Not much is known about the life of Li Bai (Li Po), one of the greatest Tang poets. He was married four times but seems never to have settled down. He was known as an iconoclast in his poetry and his life, and was said to have drowned, falling from a boat while trying drunkenly to embrace the reflected image of the moon. The translator, the novelist and poet Vikram Seth, lived and studied for several years in China.

110 **The Beautiful Toilet** Ezra Pound's title for the second of 'Nineteen Old Poems of the Han'. Pound described the Chinese poems in his 1915 collection *Cathay* as being 'for the most part from the Chinese of Rihaku [Li Bai], from the notes of the late

Ernest Fenollosa, and the decipherings of the Professors Mori and Ariga.' Pound's translations often differ from others; Pound's 'blue' grass is usually 'green'; his 'courtesan' is described in other versions as 'a dancing-house girl'; and the 'sot' who abandons her is a 'wanderer' who fails to return home. Pound's translations had a major influence on other poets, especially his close friend William Carlos Williams and his fellow Imagists H.D. [Hilda Doolittle], T. E. Hulme and Richard Aldington.

Born in Idaho in 1885, Pound lived in London from 1908 to 1920; he worked briefly as a secretary to W. B.Yeats and helped T. S. Eliot to knock 'The Waste Land' into shape, thus producing in a manageable form one of the seminal poems of the twentieth century. Pound's major work, the 'Cantos', demonstrates the influence of Chinese poetry on Pound's own writing:

> Autumn moon; hills rise about lakes
> against sunset

> Evening is like a curtain of cloud,
> a blur above ripples; and through it
> sharp long spikes of the cinnamon,
> a cold tune amid reeds.
> Behind hill the monk's bell
> borne on the wind.
> Sail passed here in April; may return in October
> Boat fades in silver; slowly;
> Sun blaze alone on the river.

(Canto 49, lines 7–17)

112 **The Red Cockatoo** Arthur Waley (1889-1966) taught himself Chinese and Japanese while working as Assistant Keeper of Oriental Prints and Manuscripts at the British Museum. Although he never visited the Far East, his elegant translations did much to popularise Chinese classical poetry among a large readership. He wrote a life of Po Chü-i, a much-loved second-generation Tang poet, and trans-

lated many of his poems. This lyric, both charming and chilling, shows us how little life has changed since the ninth century.

113 **New Year 1933** Lu Xun, the pen name of Chou Shu-jen, was celebrated for his fiction and essays and his translations from Western authors. In 1930 he founded the League of Left-Wing Writers. His classical verses use traditional forms and images, often with a biting satirical edge. An inscription to *Call to Arms*, his book of short stories, reflects his view of the writer's function:

> Take up the pen: fall into the net of law;
> Resist the times: offend popular sentiments.
> Accumulated abuse can dissolve the bones,
> And so, one gives voice to the empty page.
>
> (*translated by* WILLIAM R. SCHULTZ)

The International Settlement in Shanghai combined British and American concessions granted to foreign trading interests after the First Opium War (1842); it was returned to Chinese control in 1927. Mahjong was the popular board game played by wives of wealthy foreign and Chinese residents.

114 **'When I have fears that I may cease to be'** This sonnet was written shortly after Keats had given Leigh Hunt the first book of his long poem 'Endymion'. The young poet had been dismayed by Hunt's dismissive reaction; he described the language as being 'too high-flown'.

At this time, in January 1818, Keats's younger brother Tom was already showing signs of the tubercular illness that was to kill him by the end of the year. Keats's fears were well founded. As a trained apothecary and a former medical student at Guy's Hospital, he knew how contagious the disease was. Within three years of writing the sonnet, at the age of only 25, Keats died of consumption in Rome, where he had gone in a last desperate search for health.

The 'fair creature of an hour' does not refer to his great love Fanny Brawne, whom Keats had yet to meet, but to a young woman, briefly glimpsed, whose beauty had stirred his imagination.

116 **Birch Canoe** Carter Revard grew up as a poor Oklahoma farm boy during the Depression. He became a medieval scholar and is a distinguished Native American poet. In *Winning the Dust Bowl* he writes about his personal variation on the Old English riddle: 'I picked up the riddle form when I was getting the BA in English at Oxford University, and years later when I used it to let a Birch Canoe tell its story, I came to understand that this was also my story: the bringing into being of a mixed self, afloat between cultures and times, between heaven and earth, between North America and Europe – another way of being 'transported' into and through time.'

ACKNOWLEDGEMENTS

Patience Agbabi: 'The London Eye', © Patience Agbabi. Reprinted by permission of the author.

Amna Ahmed: 'Dockside', © Amna Ahmed 2002. Reprinted by permission of the author.

Rafael Alberti: 'The waves, blue walls', original Spanish edition 'Murallas azules, olas' from *Marinero en Tierra*, 1924, © Rafael Alberti, El Alba del Alhelí S.L.,1924. Reprinted by permission of Agencia Literaria Carmen Balcells. English translation © Mark Strand. Reprinted by permission of the translator.

Beverly Allen: 'The Aegean' by Maria Luisa Spaziani, English translation © Beverly Allen. Reprinted by permission of the translator.

Moniza Alvi: 'Indian Cooking' from *Carrying My Wife*, © Moniza Alvi 2000. Reprinted by permission of Bloodaxe Books.

Earle Birney: 'giovanni caboto/john cabot' from *Rag & Bone Shop*, © Earle Birney 1971. Reprinted by permission of McClelland & Stewart, the Canadian Publishers.

Yves Bonnefoy: 'Let a place be made', original French edition from *Du Mouvement et de l'immobilité de Douve*, © Yves Bonnefoy. Reprinted by permission of Mercure de France. English translation © Anthony Rudolf. Reprinted by permission of the translator.

Sophia de Mello Breyner: 'In the Poem', original Portuguese edition © Sophia de Mello Breyner, reprinted by permission of the author. English translation © Ruth Fainlight. Reprinted by permission of the translator.

Basil Bunting: 'First Book of Odes (6)' from *Complete Poems*, © Basil Bunting 2000. Reprinted by permission of Bloodaxe Books.

Ernesto Cardenal: 'On Lake Nicaragua' from *Apocalypse and Other Poems* (1977), © Ernesto Cardenal 1977. Reprinted by permission of New Directions.

Faustin Charles: 'Viv', © Faustin Charles. Reprinted by permission of the author.

Kate Clanchy: 'Content' from *Samarkand* (1999), Picador, © Kate Clanchy 1999. Reprinted by permission of Macmillan London.

J. P. Clark–Bekederemo: 'Ibadan', © J. P. Bekederemo. Reprinted by permission of the author.

Merle Collins: 'Free' from *Because the Dawn Breaks!* © Merle Collins 1985. Reprinted by permission of Karia Press.

David Constantine: 'Optimistic Little Poem' by Hans Magnus Enzensberger, English translation © David Constantine. Reprinted by permission of the translator. 'Coltsfoot and Larches' and 'Coltsfoot' from *Collected Poems*, © David Constantine 2004. Reprinted by permission of Bloodaxe Books.

Rae Dalven: 'Miracle' by Yannis Ritsos, English translation © Rae Dalven. Reprinted by permission of the translator.

John F. Deane: 'Canticle' from *Manhandling the Deity* (2003), © John F. Deane 2003. Reprinted by permission of Carcanet Press.

Annabelle Despard: 'Should You Die First', © Annabelle Despard 2001. Reprinted by permission of the author.

Philip Larkin: 'Cut Grass' from *High Windows* (1974), © Philip Larkin 1974. Reprinted by permission of Faber and Faber.

Laurie Lee: 'The Long War' from *Selected Poems* (1985), Penguin, © Laurie Lee 1985. Reprinted by permission of Peters, Fraser & Dunlop.

Herbert Lomas: 'Almost without Noticing' by Eira Stenberg, English translation © Herbert Lomas. Reprinted by permission of the translator.

Archibald MacLeish: 'Words in Time', from *Collected Poems, 1917–1982* © 1985 the Estate of Archibald MacLeish. Reprinted by permission of Houghton Mifflin Company.

Caitlin McLeod: 'Under the Stairs', © Caitlin McLeod 2002. Reprinted by permission of the author.

Louis MacNeice: 'Coda' from *Collected Poems*, Faber and Faber, © The Estate of Louis MacNeice. Reprinted by permission of David Higham Asoiates.

Jack Mapanje: 'The Palm Trees at Chigawe' from *Of Chameleons and Gods*, © Jack Mapanje 1981. Reprinted by permission of the author.

Khaled Mattawa: 'Poetry' by Saadi Youssef, English translation © Khaled Mattawa. Reprinted by permission of the author and translator.

W. S. Merwin: 'Separation' from *The Moving Target*, Atheneum, © W. S. Merwin 1963. Reprinted by permission of the Wylie Agency.

Czeslaw Milosz: 'And Yet the Books' from *The Collected Poems 1931–1987*, Penguin 1988, © Czeslaw Milosz Royalties 1988. English translation © the author and Robert Hass. Reprinted by permission of Ecco Press.

Marianne Moore: 'I May, I Might, I Must' from *Complete Poems*, Faber and Faber, © Marianne Moore. Reprinted by permission of Faber and Faber.

Dom Moraes: 'Architecture' from *Collected Poems 1957–1987*, © Dom Moraes. Reprinted by permission of Penguin Books India.

Frank O'Hara: 'Animals' from *Selected Poems* (1991), © Frank O'Hara 1991. Reprinted by permission of Carcanet Press.

Sharon Olds: 'The Two Apes of Brueghel' by Wisława Szymborska, English translation by Grazyna Drabik and Sharon Olds, © Quarterly Review of Literature.

Dorothy Parker: 'One Perfect Rose' from *The Best of Dorothy Parker*, Gerald Duckworth. Reprinted by permission of Gerald Duckworth.

Don Paterson: 'Web' from *Landing Light* (2003), Faber and Faber,© Don Paterson 2003. Reprinted by permission of Faber and Faber.

Anne Pennington: 'Belgrade' by Vasko Popa. English translation © Anne Pennington. Reprinted by permission of Anvil Press.

Vasko Popa: 'Belgrade' from *Collected Poems*, translated by Anne Pennington (1997), Anvil Press. Reprinted by permission of Anvil Press.

Ezra Pound: 'The Beautiful Toilet', Anon. English translation © Ezra Pound. Reprinted by permission of Faber and Faber. 'Canto 49' (lines 7-17) © Ezra Pound. Reprinted by permission of Faber and Faber.

Qian Xi Teng: 'The End of Every Field', © Qian Xi Teng 2002. Reprinted by permission of the author.

Kathleen Raine: 'Dream' from *Selected Poems* (1988), © Kathleen Raine 1988. Reprinted by permission of Golgonooza Press and Brian Keeble, Literary Executor to The Estate of Kathleen Raine.

INDEX OF POETS
AND TRANSLATORS

INDEX OF FIRST LINES

141

A NOTE OF THANKS

First and foremost we would like to thank London Underground, which has supported our programme with tact and understanding since the start. We also receive generous support from Arts Council England and the British Council, which distributes posters to its offices across the world.

Thanks for special projects are due to the Foreign and Commonwealth Office, the Polish Cultural Institute, and the former Minister for Europe, Denis MacShane, a warm advocate for poetry. The Poetry Society education staff were instrumental in organising two displays of poems by young poets.

We have benefited from the unfailing courtesy of Librarians at the British Library, Magdalene College Cambridge, the Peterborough Museum & Art Gallery, British Museum Prints & Drawings, the John Murray Archive, the Poetry Library (South Bank Centre) and the Barbican Library.

It has been a pleasure to work with Yukki Yaura, creator of original calligraphy in an ancient tradition, and with Laurie Lipton, who brought the Polynesian god A'a to life in her beautifully crafted drawing. For the special display of Chinese poems we are grateful to the master calligrapher Qu Lei Lei and to Frances Wood, Curator of Chinese Books and Manuscripts at the British Library. Tom Davidson has designed our posters since 1989, and continues to weather last-minute crises with unflappable good humour. Barry Holmes, our genial editor, has provided support and counsel, relishing the task of returning Poems on the Underground to the printed page whence they came.

We receive welcome advice from friends and fellow writers, as well as the poetry-loving public. To all, our thanks.

Readers may like to know that posters are available from London's Transport Museum and the Poetry Society. Information about our programme is carried on the websites of Transport for London, the Poetry Society and the British Council.

THE EDITORS

Gerard Benson, Poems on the Underground's only Londoner by birth, now commutes from Bradford for meetings with his two colleagues. He has earned his living as lecturer, labourer, waiter, window cleaner, sailor and actor (to mention but a few), but now mainly subsists as a writer, editor and speaker of poetry. In 1994 he was poet-in-residence at the Wordsworth Trust; and in 2004 judged poetry competitions for Peterloo Press and The Poetry Business. His most recent book (for children), *Omba Bolomba*, is delightfully illustrated by his wife, Catherine. They are both Quakers.

Judith Chernaik grew up in New York City and in 1972 moved with her husband and children to London, where she has lived ever since. She has loved English poetry since coming across *A Child's Garden of Verses* as a girl of seven. But she is incurably addicted to prose, and has written four novels as well as a study of Shelley's lyrics. She has lectured here and there, and written on subjects as diverse as a Welsh primary school, the London Library, boredom in Brooklyn, poetry and politics, music and madness. She is currently working on a novel about Schumann's last years.

Cicely Herbert knows many poems by heart. She learned Shelley's 'Ode to the West Wind' in less than an hour in a greenhouse in Sidcup and became a Barrow Poet. The past has caught up with her in the form of the re-release in Australia of an 80s hit record, 'The Pheasant Plucker's Song', in which she portrays the eponymous hero's wife, with Gerard Benson singing the role of his friend, to music by Bafta Award-winning composer Jim Parker. This song can be heard on a compilation album entitled 'Funny Peculiar'. Her advice to the ambitious is simply: 'Learn poems and the world is your oyster.'